Wildflower Poems

PATRICIA BRAWLEY

Copyright © 2023 by Patricia Brawley.

ISBN: 979-8-8909-0195-8 (sc)
ISBN: 979-8-8909-0196-5 (eb)

All rights reserved. No part of this book may be reproduced or transmitted in any form or by any means, electronic or mechanical, including photocopying, recording, or by any information storage and retrieval system, without permission in writing from the copyright owner.

The views expressed in this work are solely those of the author and do not necessarily reflect the views of the publisher, and the publisher hereby disclaims any responsibility for them.

EXPRESSO
Executive Center 777, Dunsmuir Street Vancouver, BC V71K4
1-888-721-0662 ext 101
info@expressopublishing.com

Note:

These poems are organic, much like wildflower seeds that blow through the air, words, images and themes formed in my thoughts. They are not pretty, all planted in-a-row poems. The are mostly from seeds of my own life but some come from doing therapy many years and hearing stories, dreams of others. You can imagine that petal hear and there are sourced from their lives and the impressions they made on me.

They are all gifts of the air.

Table of Contents

The Gifts of Air 1
Who Goes There? 2
Mommie, Mommie, I Can't Find A Place For My Voice 4
A Child Is Born... 7
Sins of the Mother.. 8
Wild Flowers in a White Paper Cup 9
Message.. 11
Living With Dying 12
The Wait... 14
The Day My Nightmare Died (my cat) 15
Postcard From The Edge 16
Eternity Matters.. 17
Enemy Lines 19
Metastisis 20
Waiting Rooms 21
Still Life 22
Omen – part 1 23
Omen – part II 24
Clouds 25
Unraveling 26
Widow 27
Alone 28
I Can't Do This.. 29
Crazy 30
Storm Cloud 31
Two Weeks After Your Death... 32
The Favorite Tree in the Park 33
Emergency Contact 34
Lists 35

At Least 36
Measuring Time 37
Affirmations 38
What To Do With Myself 39
Time 40
Widow at the Window 41
Downsizing Surprise 43

The Gifts of Air

People say things like
'love is in the air' and
'I can smell rain in the air.'

People say they get ideas
out of thin air
Some people get the big Ah-Ha!
Like Einstein or poets.

The air we breathe-the same air that
Flows through the Universe
Seems laden with gifts.

This air, the breath of life,
The keeper of the soul.
The last breath returning to the Cosmos.

Is it any wonder Yogis, Mystics, and Healers
talk about Deep Breathing?

Who Goes There?

Who goes there?
Are you the ghost of writer's block?
Come to scare me away from the pen?

Who goes there?
Are you reincarnated from sacred text
holding secrets until you deem
I am worthy of knowing?

Do you not know I am woman?
I wait, unknowing, and uncertain.
Sidling up to my heart of fear,
facing truth when it comes.

The words have to be there.
Everything is connected
from the horizon of silence
tethered to the spoken word.

Why do you guard them fiercely?
As though if one word comes through
to the poet, a deluge of words will deplete you.

There's no scarcity --except for this ecology
of wordlessness.

Who goes there?
When I write
Will I become a ghost, too?
Hovering over another soul
Waiting for her muse?

Not knowing she too
will be the one asking
'Who goes there?'

Mommie, Mommie, I Can't Find A Place For My Voice

She is 4-years-old.

She's dressed herself in the frock her mother made,
skirt smoothed down,
buckled sandals on her little feet.
Hair pinned with a barrette,
face washed, eyes scared.
Listening.

She stands at the end of her made-up bed that she did herself.
She can almost see herself in the floor she shines,
pushing the dust mop over and over,
every day.
Her few toys are out of sight,
line up on the closet floor
waiting to be rescued.

Did I tell you she is 4-years-old?

Hush up now. Be quiet.
Go clean your room.
Leave Mommie alone.
'Go clean your room' is the lullaby
her mother sings to her
Every day.

Is it any wonder
she learns her voice
is something
to put away?

How long will she be 4-years-old?

II

Did I tell you she is 44-years-old?

Sobbing, she tells her therapist
about her childhood.
When she hoped for love and felt none.
How she's tried to be good
and please and work hard.

She has replayed this theme
like an old song in every relationship.
Hush up. Clean the house.
Her life on hold, all lined up
Waiting to be rescued.

She's done waiting.

A journa, her therapist says
will help her find her voice.
Silently, writing from her heart
She begins.

Words drop to the page,
Snapshots of her life,
like wet clothes on a clothes line,
Heavy.

Crayons, her therapist says,
will help her play, draw her feelings.
She scribbles faces.
They are all screaming.

Photography, her therpist says,
will bring beauty into her world.
She aims the camera
Closets and cages are her still life.

A gallery displays her art. She is exposed.
Finally seen and heard without saying a word.
A lifetime ago, she remembers it all now.
She was 4-years-old.
.
A lifetime ahead to sing her own song.

A Child Is Born

A child is born.
She has a mother and father.
They never become parents.

A child is born.
She is alone.
Angels tend her.
Every missed love note
Formed a thorn in her heart.

A Child is born.
Missed birthdays
overlooked celebrations
Dismissed accomplishments
Entice the throns to move
Deeper.

A Child is Born.
Thorns hurt forever.
They never become parents.
Angels mourn for her.

Sins of the Mother

In the dream, his silver colored car
Remind him of a crumpled spaceship
By the road's edge.
Wrecked but like an oragami
Piece of art ready to pop back whole.
Like nothing had happened.

In the dream, the family is trapped
inside the car. They are exhausted
From the struggle to be free.
They are alive but something
Is dead.

In the dream, they see her-
His wife, their mother.
She has escaped the wreck
And found the highway.

In the dream, the children
Are convinced she's going for help.
She will return for them.

In the dream, he watches her
Maternal=shaped figure walk
Resolutely away from them.
Never looking back.

In the dream, he wonders what drew her
To repeat the story of her mother leaving her?
Om the dream, she is free wile others
Struggle to exist alongside abandonment.

And yet, he says she is beautiful.

Wild Flowers in a White Paper Cup

Love came when I was too young
amd you were too old.
Knowing glances, stolen kisses, and sweet talk
kindled a fire that would not die
but could not burn bright.
Still, we had a glimpse into the well.

In the morning, you brought
wild flowers in a white paper cup
and placed them on your desk.
Flowers, like love, that grew with
no rhyme or reason. Colorful,
prone to disapproval. Mowed over.

By end of day, it was okay to
give them as a gift with the excuse
of not throwing them away.
Wild flowers that grew
not to please or look a certain way.
Rescued, treasured, and saved.

Like seeds carried by wind, our lives drifted
and grew again in other places, other times.
Life was mired in ordinary and good.
Love was still there when I was older
and you were not too old and
fate stunned us with chance.

Our lives were jangled awake.
You came. You brought me
wild flowers in a white paper cup
and I cried.

Plans were made, our lives re-imagined.
Wilted flowers grew strong again.
And then the message....
You told me you were dying.
"Don't come, you said.
It's too far; it's too late".

The mourning was unrelenting.
I thought the flowers died.

Now, I'm old and you've been gone
thirty years. No matter, it's time to make the journey.
It's time to write the last page in my diary.

With miles behind me
and a full moon lighting my way,
I'm ready to release the weight of death.

A white skirt brushes my ankles
as I glide down the aisle of tombstones
with the heat of a bride ready to take her vow,
and gently place
wild flowers in a white paper cup
upon your grave.

Message

'I am always with you. I am always with you.'
I hear this in my mind.
'I only died. I never left you.
We sleep together every night.'

I want to know: when you died
Did a god or goddess meet you?
Take you to a heavenly place?
Heal your body?
Is it really paradise? Or, a dark
Shadow of life? Or, just dark.

I hope you were cared for,
that you were excited to be the new guest!
Seated amongst your heroes and ancestors.

Wait for me. Leave me a seat at the table,
but, not just yet.

Living With Dying

You're a thief!
You take money,
Life,
Thoughts
Blood.

When I was a mass of swirling matter
Threads matching with other threads
Cells Forming in the womv.
Were you with me then?

When I was born and ran and played
Carefree and well.
Were you with me then?
Where did you hide?

Have we played hind-and-seek
all my life?
Why wait to say 'Boo!"
in my sixties?

You say you showed your face
witih symptoms of thirst.
Really?
That's not fair.

I have to guess your name.
I didn't know you were in the game,
Were you my shadow-
A partner I didn't choose?

Or did genetic tendrils
Come out of the womb soup
To seep into my body
Unannounced?

The Wait

I've been waiting for you.
My mother told me for 60 years
You would come.
But nobody believes that.

You came to see my father
and my grandfather
and all his brothers and sisters.
But, I am special.

You came in silence like a stranger
Walking through my home
When I was not there.
I sensed your presence.
Something's just not right.

We slept together, so close
You snuggled to fit my body
And eased into my flesh
Yet, I didn't know you were there.

How can I wait for you and
Not see you when you arrive?
How do I greet you when you
Become visible to me?

How will you change my life?
How do I say your name and
Introduce you to my friends?

They won't like you.
Diabetes Mellitus Type Two.

The Day My Nightmare Died (my cat)

You lay belly to belly, heart to heart
As I rocked you by the fireplace
And lovingly fed you sugar milk
Knowing my attempt would
Not block Death's calling.

Since a foundling kitten, you had
A wild spirit. Not today.
You are a breath away from death
and the wildness had left.
Reducing us to beings who've shared a life.

Memories: you were so big and bad during the day
At nighttime, you snuggled close,
Like a kitten looking for a lost mother.
Now, in the ebbing light of life, I feel your paws
Searching for her, searching for me.
I will long for that again. I will long for
Everything about you.

The Universe mirrors our day.
Snowy weather brings a power outage.
The house, me, and you are cold.
Snow falls gently, blanketing the earth.
As a loving mother covers her child.

Silent Night is Here.

Postcard From The Edge

When I'm an old woman,
older than me,
Memories of driving the zig=zag lane
to the house on Hurricane point
(what a name!)
will remind me of cliff dwellers,
living on the edge of time,
free to see the ocean and
melt away
into memories
that waft like the tides
til the next edge of life.

Eternity Matters

I'm here to evaluate, Miss…, I tell the nurse.
"She's 90, gesturing
toward the exit door,
She waits there. Every day."

I approach. She turns.
I glimpse her younger beauty
now reddened with rouge.,

In her clear light voice, she says
"I'm waiting for the taxi
to take me to my new home.'

Is she telling the truth?
Or, living her truth?
Does it matter?
When does eternity begin?
Not at death, but now.

In fixing her gaze on the future
Does she feel the joy of hope or
miss her mundane life?
Oh, the power of faith
That ekes from the mind at old age.

Oh, the power of faith
to trust the known but
Unseen as true, at any age.

Faith is not worthless
Hope is not frivolous
Reason has to fight for sight.

Lest we slip into our dream
of waiting for the taxi.

Enemy Lines

Where are they? The top of a hill?
A hole in the ground? Or in a mountain cave?

Invisible lines lure soldiers toward them,
sink them to baser instincts
to life out a noir story that has no ending
and a miserable plot.

Those who live have nor survived.
They can't yet know they are tethered
to every line they inched toward,
revisited in their nightmares.

It the airport I wait for you.
You came home alone, no parades.
I'm holding the baby you've never seen.
I see you. The skinny boy returned a man.

Enemy lines rearranged your face.
A furrowed brow molded from war.
We didn't know then how much you had changed
how sick you would become.

Taps played. I stood by your grave
wondering who made the fatal decisions
That killed you.

Did their faces mirror the thousands of faces
haunted by enemy lines?
Or did the notion of peace wash deep into flesh
whey they found courage

To save us.

Metastisis

A word with energy like
you could dance to it with
stomping feet and bells in your hands.

I Googled the word.
My mind froze as
The message of doom
Made itself known.
No dancing to the reality of
metastisis.

I felt the first scare
The first imagined aloneness
And then he came into
The kitchen feeling chipper
And I welcomed relief.

Maybe we can slow dance.

Waiting Rooms

The first week of doctor's waiting rooms
People shuffling, rolling along
Still trying to get well.
So many decisions
To pick one with hope.
Impermanence in Neon Lights.

Still Life

A collection of things not alive
Arranged for the artist to paint
She controls how things fit.
There is a sense of order.
Until a bit of cancerous tissue
Invades the scene
Alive – not belonging to my Still Life.

Omen – part 1

Today it rains
Setting the scene
Of departure.
Traveling to hear
What a surgeon
Has to say.

Today it rains,
Thunders the unspoken
Fears in my mind.
Reveals my broken heart
As we go forth toward the unknown
Looking for hope.

Omen – part II

The trip to the doctor starts, then stops.
The dashboard signals
Not enough air in a tire.
Reminding me about air (breath)- not enough.
We change cars.
Then, we need an umbrella
And rain jacket
And, close the gate, too.
We try to make things safe.
Departure. The closer we get
The more it rains and fogs
My vision, making it hard to
See my lane.
And, along the way
He holds out his left hand
For me to see he's lost
His wedding ring.

What else?

Clouds

The clouds don't move.
Sitting for hours in the ICU waiting room
Looking through the slatted window blinds
I see the blue sky and white fluffy clouds.

Realizing, with a start,
The clouds don't move. It's as though
I am looking at a painting.
Still Life.
Even the heavens reflect
Stillness, sitting, waiting.
Hovering between life and clouds.

Unraveling

All the women in my family sewed
As was needed and expected.
My mother elevated hers
to creative art;
mine never measured up
but there were moments
and my daughter brought
creative sewing back to our history.

When you learn how to
Piece, pin, and stitch
It feels complete -like a life.
When cancer unravels a life
There is an attempt to
Stitch it back in place
But it continues to unravel
Gaining momentum until
All you can do is witness.

Widow

His first words of the day
"you're going to be a widow today."
I drop my head and then tell him
I don't think so but if it happens
Promise me you will wait for me
And if I go first, I will wait for you.
We will find each other.
I love you.

Alone

While you are in the hospital it hits me –
This is what's it's like – living alone.
But, I'm not ready to believe that.

I Can't Do This

Looking for pictures for your obituary
I see your life when you were
Alive, well and happy.

I wash the clothes you
Wore to the hospital
I put away your Kleenex, flashlight, Swiss Army knife-
Things you will need.

Crazy

I reach my arms toward the heavens
Hoping you will join me
Like in Michalangelo's painting
Reaching for the heavens.

Storm Cloud

Grief. It's like standing underneath a storm cloud.
With no warning the rain comes.
On the inside,
Waves of emotion starting in my heart
Traveling to my gut.

Two Weeks After Your Death

The sun shines on my
sorrowed face
The birds sing to ears
that do not hear.

The Favorite Tree in the Park

Does the tree remember him
whizzing by on
his electric bicycle like a
happy boy?

Would Tree allow him
to rest there? In the green
he loved? Listening for
the train?

Memories growing into the bark
Tears, just tears.

Emergency Contact

Filling out forms, the nurse asks-
Who is your emergency contact?
The question stuns. I struggle
to remember my daughter's name.

One more loss – like the dried
flowers in a vase I saved from
my birthday gift.

No more flowers,
Christmas presents, restaurant meals.
Emergency Contact has been
taken from me.

Lists

Sometime after you're gone
My attention turns to things
You have given me: the dried
Flowers in the vase you gave
For my birthday. I save some of them.

This prompts the list:
I'll never get birthday flowers again;
I'll never get roses and candy for Valentines again
I'll never get a Christmas present from you
I'll never have a date for eating out again
I'll never have a cheerleader and hear 'terrific!" from you again

Of course I recognize this is selfish and I began making lists for you
You'll never listen to your loved music again
You'll never hear your children and grandchildren's voices again
You'll never ride your e bike, like a boy, through the neighborhood
You'll never go to the grocery store which always brought a joy to you
You'll never go to Canada again.

I quit complaining about weather: yes, it is cold
And the wind flushes my cheeks but I think
What you wouldn't give to have one moment of cold
Air on your cheek. To live for one more moment.

At Least

Then begins the habit of comparison and making up stories
At least: you weren't murdered,
At least you didn't run off
At least you grew old
At least you didn't live in the nursing home
At least you left things in order
At least our last words to each other
Were I love you. At least you heard
Words of love during the time you
Were unconscious and we thought you could still hear.
At least I was holding your hand till the last heartbeat.
At least you felt my hands behind your neck, cradling your head.
At least you were kissed on your way to the stars.

Measuring Time

Dates are a part of my life.
Paperwork, accounting, calendars prompt me to think
to myself "he was alive then" or
'we didn't have a clue he would die then"
"he was healthy then, we thought" or
"he was getting sick then" and "he was worried then"
And then "he was gone by then."

As if there is Before Death and After Death
divisions in the calendar.
I so wish I could erase it all.

Affirmations

Positive affirmations promise
to uplift and craft your day; keep
your mind on your dreams.

How do you create a positive
affirmation about being a widow?
"I am a creative happy widow?"
Can the word exist in any affirmation?

It seems my affirmations
skirt around this word, this
new status.
I feel the energy of positive words -
like creative, traveler, poet –
but how do I affirm
widowhood.

A Koan.

What To Do With Myself

I don't know what to do with myself
What did I used to do
When I didn't feel this way?

Wandering through the rooms
we shared
I feel lost
Looking for some part of me
that's vanished
Did you take it with you?

I'm putting together a new self
One that smiles to hide my
screams.
When will I feel "like my old self" again?

Time

I got my hair done yesterday
I missed hearing your compliments
about the new cut, color, style.
Yesterday, there was no need to rush
home or anywhere.
I have time now.
Time to loiter, dally about.
I feel adrift. You were my
anchor.

I hammered a nail yesterday early
The time didn't matter. No one to
wake.

Widow at the Window

When I was a girl, living in an old house
a chimney sweep fell into the unused fireplace
and we were both scared!

The Chimney sweep frantically flew
around the room, blinded no doubt
by the light. I ran screaming
for my mother.

When you died, I became a Chimney sweep.
I fell down the shaft, black and covered in soot
Made of sadness and memories.
I flew toward the window only to
bang my beak on the glass hard.
In pain, I flew there over and over
Until exhaustion forced me to sit
still on the floor with my racing heart.
No way out.

The scared child tips to the door
and opens it wide
There is a threshold and a world
I don't recognize.

I do not fly yet.
I walk toward the open door
Look toward the heavens
and soar. Still black and sooty
I'm out, free.

I don't know where I will land
or how far I will go
It will be a new place, even a new chimney
and I will fall again.

Downsizing Surprise

It was time.
I downsized.
Loved stuff and old rituals
squeezed into new spaces.
I still brewed morning coffee and
looked out the kitchen window.
Now, it is a different view and
one I do not like.

Ropes of dried vines hung from
the neighbor's tree behind my fence.
The neighbor had downsized too, moved away,
Maybe I could convince a tree trimmer
to whack out the dried vines.
This began the morning internal dialog, story after story
Leaving me feeling helpless.

Why hadn't I looked out the window before choosing this house?
Who tells you to do that?

Spring came and the joke was on me.
I still brewed coffee and looked out the window.
One morning I couldn't believe my eyes!
The vines, which I thought were dead, were alive!
Beautiful purple Wisteria now cascaded and draped
through the tree to my fence. Breathtaking.

I had wasted time judging nature and feeling helpless
to fix something that was already perfect.
Another Life lesson.

Ordinary Genius
Springs From
Blue Thin Air

www.ingramcontent.com/pod-product-compliance
Lightning Source LLC
LaVergne TN
LVHW041222080526
838199LV00082B/2019